£29

ILLUMINATIONS

Illuminations

A Ro-Mlen Alphabet

Written and Illustrated by Janice Davis Civen

Dodd, Mead & Company · New York

Published by Dodd, Mead & Company, Inc.
79 Madison Avenue, New York, N.Y. 10016
Distributed in Canada by
McClelland and Stewart Limited, Toronto
Photography by Orville Crane
Printed in Hong Kong by South China Printing Company
Designed by Abe Lerner
First Edition   SC984

Library of Congress Cataloging in Publication Data

Civen, Janice Davis.
      Illuminations : a Ro-mlen alphabet.

      1. Civen, Janice Davis.   2. Alphabets in art.
I. Title.
ND3410.C5A4   1984   745.6'7'0924   84-8009
ISBN 0-396-08176-2

PREFACE

§ The Text

The text of *Illuminations* consists of twenty-six brief commentaries, one on each of twenty-six words arranged alphabetically from A to Z. These commentaries are not intended to be literal definitions of the words but rather observations of an intuitive nature, often expressed in poetic terms. They are attempts to set down insights into reality as I have comprehended it at certain points in my life; and though they may be limited by my limitations, I hope that they express in some measure the depth, truth, and beauty of the inner realms.

§ The Illustrations

As the text came to me and I wrote it down, I envisioned each commentary as being profusely illustrated in the style of the old illuminated manuscripts. In order to capture the sense and feeling of that kind of illustration, I have studied and drawn freely from the designs and styles of such manuscripts— sometimes copying particular letters, borders, and patterns quite closely, often adapting them to the needs of the text and mingling them overall with ideas and inspirations of my own.

I would like to acknowledge the following books in particular as the source of many of the artistic inspirations in *Illuminations*. For full-color reproductions, I am much indebted to *The Hours of Catherine of Cleves* and *The Visconti Hours*, both published by George Braziller of New York. For black-and-white alphabets and for line drawings of intricate manuscript initials that date back many centuries I am particularly indebted to *Decorative Alphabets and Initials*, edited by Alexander Nesbitt, published by Dover Publications of New York.

As well as thanking those who have made these works of art available to us, I would like to thank the unknown masters who produced the beautiful manuscripts of old and who have been my teachers, however unknowingly, as I worked on the paintings for this text.

§ The Title

The title *Illuminations: A Ro-Mlen Alphabet* came about in this way. Often, when I am engaged in some contemplative activity—painting, meditating, walking on a beach, and so on—my mind travels to an imaginary place which I call *Ro-Mlen*. I think of *Ro-Mlen* as an other-worldly kingdom of truth and beauty and, for me, it is a world of creative inspiration and inner refreshment.

Ro-Mlen is the origin of, and inspiration for, both the text and the paintings in this book.

Janice Davis Civen

ILLUMINATIONS

A is for ANSWERS

A is for **Answers**

ANSWERS are something without any boundaries.

They cannot be contained, they can only be pursued.

An answer achieved is a step on the path of Action-Being. Questions are like stones on that path. Answers are the movement that carries us from one stone to the next. If we pay the stone too much concentration it is as if we are absorbed into it and feel that it constricts around us in our struggle.

Answers are the entry of Divine Breath into the area of constriction. They loose an energy of buoyant life that expands the boundaries of comprehension.

Answers are not stopping places—they are doorways into new thought.

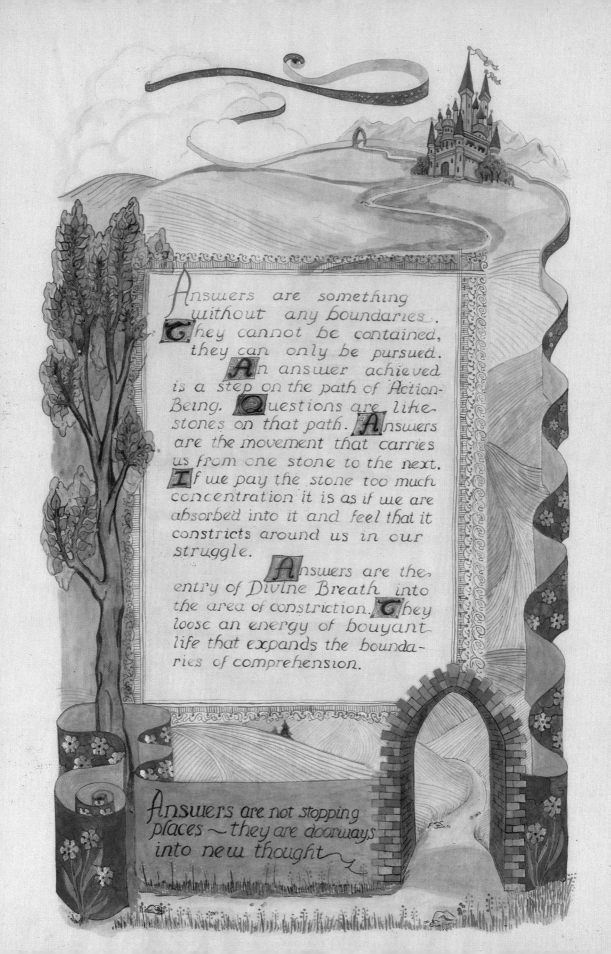

Answers are something without any boundaries. They cannot be contained, they can only be pursued. An answer achieved is a step on the path of Action-Being. Questions are like stones on that path. Answers are the movement that carries us from one stone to the next. If we pay the stone too much concentration it is as if we are absorbed into it and feel that it constricts around us in our struggle.

Answers are the entry of Divine Breath into the area of constriction. They loose an energy of bouyant life that expands the boundaries of comprehension.

Answers are not stopping places — they are doorways into new thought —

B is for BLESSEDNESS

B is for
Blue
and
has

BLESSEDNESS is not, as many think, the reward of practicing virtue. Rather, blessedness is the very soil in which all living things are sown, and from which they grow.

Nothing is, that is not rooted in blessedness; nothing is transformed, that it goes not to another state of blessedness.

The practice of virtue is an exercise by which our eyes are opened to see—not only whence we come and where we go, but where we at the moment stand.

Blessedness is the very stuff of being; to be is to be blessed.

Blessedness is not, as many think, the reward of practicing virtue. Rather, blessedness is the very soil in which all living things are sown, and from which they grow.

Nothing is, that is not rooted in blessedness; nothing is transformed, that it goes not to another state of blessedness.

The practice of virtue is an exercise by which our eyes are opened to see — not only whence we come and where we go, but where we at the moment stand.

Blessedness is the very stuff of being: to be is to be blessed.

C is for CHANCE

CHANCE is like a naughty child. He wears masks gay or sad, behaving like a clown. But he can only deceive other children, and it is they themselves who provide his masks.

When children tire of his games they put the masks away, to know who stands behind the façade.

Then they speak no more of chance for they have ceased playing in the shallow pools of illusion and gone on to seek the treasures of the Greater Deeps.

Chance is like a naughty child. He wears masks gay or sad, behaving like a clown. But he can only deceive other children, and it is they themselves who provide his masks.

When children tire of his games, they put the masks away, to know who stands behind the facade.

Then they speak no more of chance for they have ceased playing in the shallow pools of illusion and gone on to seek the treasures of the Greater Deeps.

D is for DUTY

is for

Duty

DUTY is the cloak that the Hidden One wears before us, lest we be overcome by a full revelation before we are made ready. Even so cloaked, His Light shines through, and thus we value Duty, honoring those who do their duty well.

It is in this striving that humankind is made ready to see a new day dawn—the Day wherein the Hidden One shall shed His cloak and stand before us—undisguised.

Then, though all is performed most perfectly, the word "duty" is not called upon, for the spontaneous action of Love is such that, where it flows in fullness, all is done well and joyously without awareness of striving.

Duty is the cloak that the Hidden One wears before us, lest we be overcome by a full revelation before we are made ready. Even so cloaked, His Light shines through, and thus we value Duty, honoring those who do their duty well.

It is in this striving that humankind is made ready to see a new day dawn—the Day wherein the Hidden One shall shed His cloak and stand before us — undisguised.

Then, though all is performed most perfectly, the word "duty" is not called upon, for the spontaneous action of Love is such that, where it flows in fullness, all is done well and joyously without awareness of striving.

E is for EGGS

E is for ECCY

An EGG is a small consciousness who has not yet known anything but darkness and yet its whole intent is its struggle to reach the light.

Thus the Divine lives in secret at the heart of every unit of Creation, and it is this innate Divine Impetus within us that leads us to break through again and again into new states of awareness. The whole of life is but a hatching from one Egg of awareness to another, greater egg—a growing out of one Egg of comprehension into another greater Egg.

All that is can be understood in terms of Eggs. If we understood an Egg, we would understand Creation.

An Egg is a small consciousness who has not yet known anything but darkness and yet its whole intent is its struggle to reach the light.

Thus the Divine lives in secret at the heart of every unit of Creation, and it is this innate Divine Impetus within us that leads us to break through again and again into new states of awareness. The whole of life is but a hatching from one Egg of awareness to another, greater Egg ~ a growing out of one Egg of comprehension into another greater Egg.

All that is can be understood in terms of Eggs. If we understood an Egg, we would understand Creation.

F is for FREEDOM

F is for FREEDOM

FREEDOM is the birthright of all that lives. There is none who cannot claim that birthright. We know a labyrinth of self-imposed restrictions, or live in chains of self-wrought chaos, yet if we will do so we can free ourselves from these bonds.

Freedom cannot be kept, nor won again once lost, without a discipline of soul, and many languish in slavery who will not embrace the effort of right discipline. When each has made the effort and disciplined his own spirit to a state of true freedom, then all other slaveries—spiritual or material—will vanish from our world.

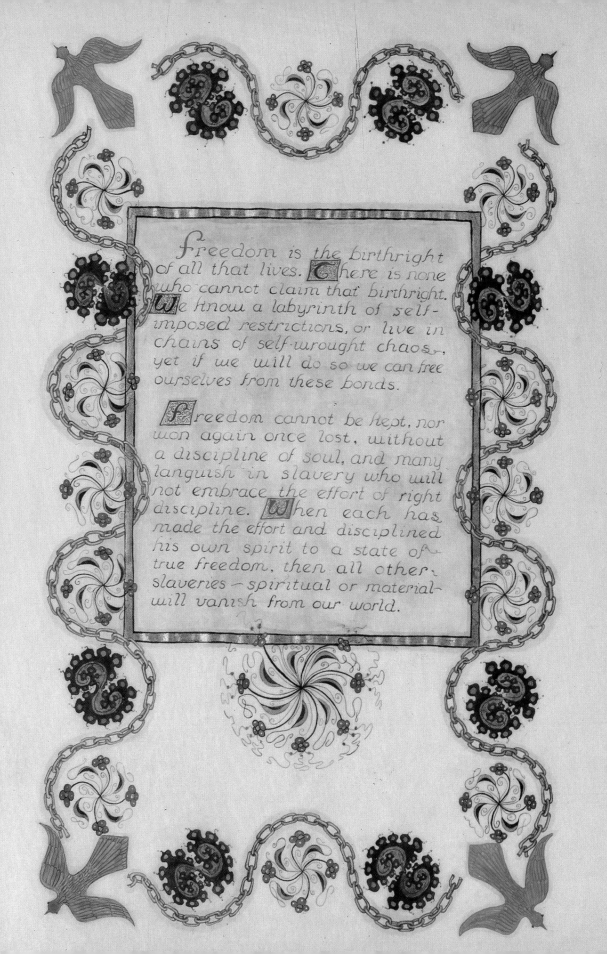

Freedom is the birthright of all that lives. There is none who cannot claim that birthright. We know a labyrinth of self-imposed restrictions, or live in chains of self-wrought chaos, yet if we will do so we can free ourselves from these bonds.

Freedom cannot be kept, nor won again once lost, without a discipline of soul, and many languish in slavery who will not embrace the effort of right discipline. When each has made the effort and disciplined his own spirit to a state of true freedom, then all other slaveries — spiritual or material — will vanish from our world.

G is for GROWTH

G is for GROWN

GROWTH is the continuing transformation through which Each (Unit of Creation) knows itself to be all, and through which the All realizes itself in the myriad manifestations of Each.

Growth is the principle of Being.

Growth is the continuing transformation through which Each (Unit of Creation) knows itself to be all, and through which the All realizes itself in the myriad manifestations of Each. Growth is the principle of Being

h is for HUMILITY

H is for humility

HUMILITY is truth, neither more nor less.

It is neither abject nor pretentious. It follows on the footsteps of those who seek the Divine Heart within— and when we find ourselves at one with All, we find Humility at our right hand.

It is said that those who give up all else for love of God will be given All.

Herein lies Humility.

Humility is truth, neither more nor less. It is neither abject nor pretentious. It follows on the footsteps of those who seek the Divine Heart within — and when we find ourselves at one with All, we find Humility at our right hand.

It is said that those who give up all else for love of God will be given All. Herein lies Humility.

I is for INTUITION

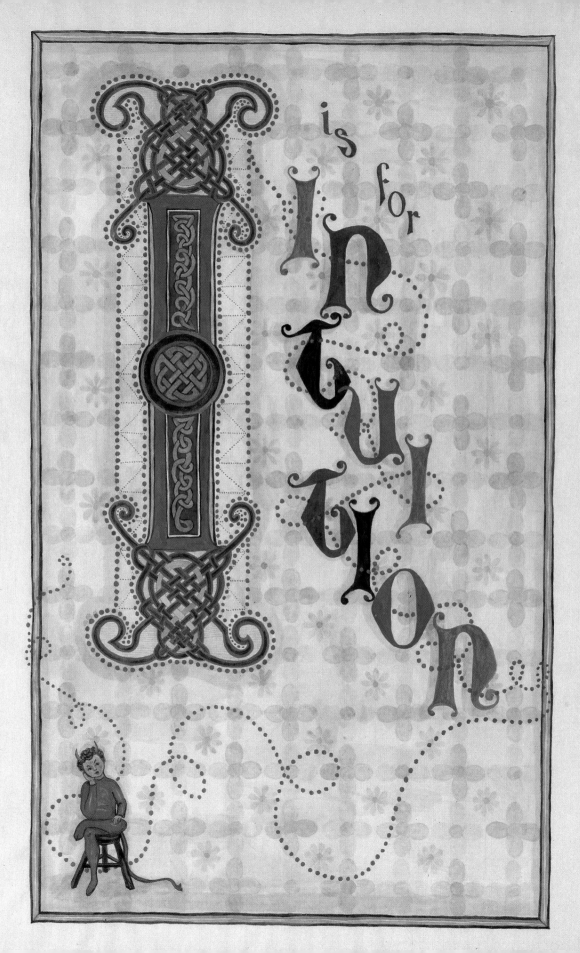

I is for Intuition

INTUITION, you might say, is the result of an Ignition of Information. Through intellect, through sensual impulse, through original imprint reinforced by life experience, the soul gathers knowledge. When, in a given area, the body of knowledge becomes full enough, it is as if a "spontaneous combustion" takes place. The result is not destruction but a high-intensity fusing together of the related knowledge-particles into a compacted form: a sort of "nugget of knowings."

This nugget has lost nothing of the original except the original form. The details of arriving at the knowledge may be hidden from the conscious mind, but the end result is the same. It is as if we had a computer replacing a cumbrous filing system—we get instant answers without being aware of the interior calculations that lead to those answers.

Intuition is not, as some suppose, opposed to intellect.

Rather, it is a refined state of the intellectual processes.

Intuition, you might say, is the result of an Ignition of Information. Through intellect, through sensual impulse, through original imprint reinforced by life experience, the soul gathers knowledge. When, in a given area, the body of knowledge becomes full enough, it is as if a "spontaneous combustion" takes place. The result is not destruction but a high-intensity fusing together of the related knowledge-particles into a compacted form: a sort of "nugget-of-knowings."

This nugget has lost nothing of the original except the original form. The details of arriving at the knowledge may be hidden from the conscious mind, but the end result is the same. It is as if we had a computer replacing a cumbrous filing system.—we get instant answers without being aware of the interior calculations that lead to those answers

Intuition is not, as some suppose, opposed to intellect. Rather, it is a refined state of the intellectual processes.

J is for JUGGLER

J is for JUGGLER

JUGGLERS are windows into Divine Activity.

The Juggler is, at once, still and in unceasing motion.

Within the Juggler's action all ever falls and ever rises, flows, turns, changes, in balance and in harmony.

Here, utter concentration is at one with utter ease. Here is the activity of Serious Delight.

Jugglers are windows into Divine Activity.

The Juggler is, at once, still and in unceasing motion.

Within the juggler's action all ever falls and ever rises, flows, turns, changes, in balance and in harmony. Here, utter concentration is at one with utter ease. Here is the activity of Serious Delight.

K is for KARMA

KARMA is the "how come?" of the universe.

Little karmas turn within greater karmas and when we ask "How come?" it may be well to look past the first answer to the second, and to look short of the first answer for the partly-answer.

Karma has a key which wise men know; the karmic wheels turn on the Staff of the Divine, but the staff itself is still.

Those who seek, in every experience, its centre of Divinity, shall find both the fullest benefits of the karma flowing around them and that Peace of God which surpasses all understanding.

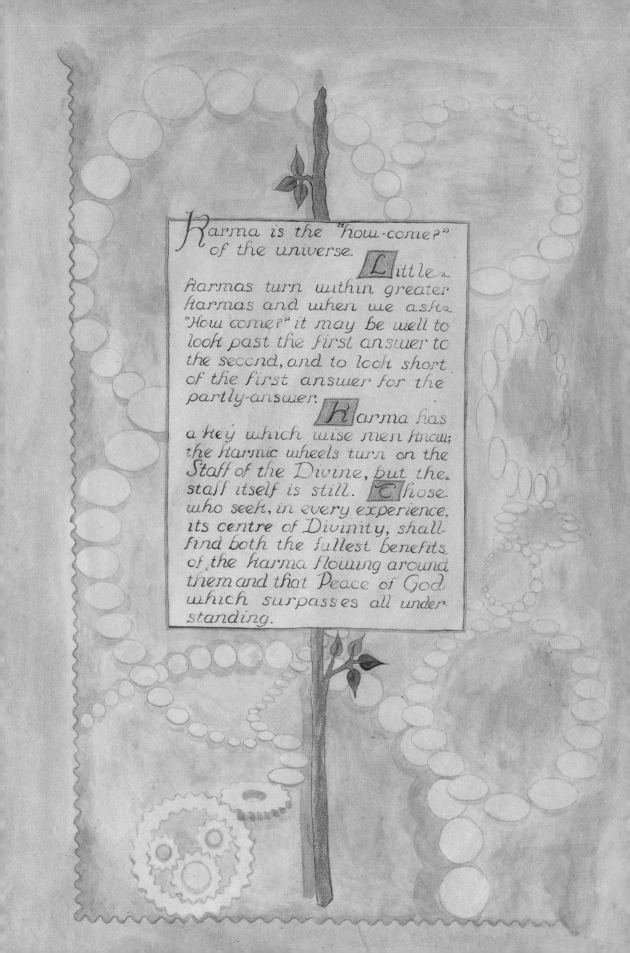

Karma is the "how-come?" of the universe. Little karmas turn within greater karmas and when we ask "How come?" it may be well to look past the first answer to the second, and to look short of the first answer for the partly-answer. Karma has a key which wise men know; the karmic wheels turn on the Staff of the Divine, but the staff itself is still. Those who seek, in every experience, its centre of Divinity, shall find both the fullest benefits of the karma flowing around them and that Peace of God which surpasses all understanding.

L is for LAW

L is for

LAMB

LAW, in its purest form, is that spontaneous action within Each that continually maintains, transforms, and interacts harmoniously with all else.

Where Love's expression is limited, Law gains concrete form increasingly, in ratio to the degree of limitation—and loses, in like degree, the spontaneous inner life which makes it workable. Then, not the law, but the inner life of the "lawmakers" is in need of reform.

In its purest form law simply *is* and needs no conscious observation.

Where Love is perfect, Law is perfect.

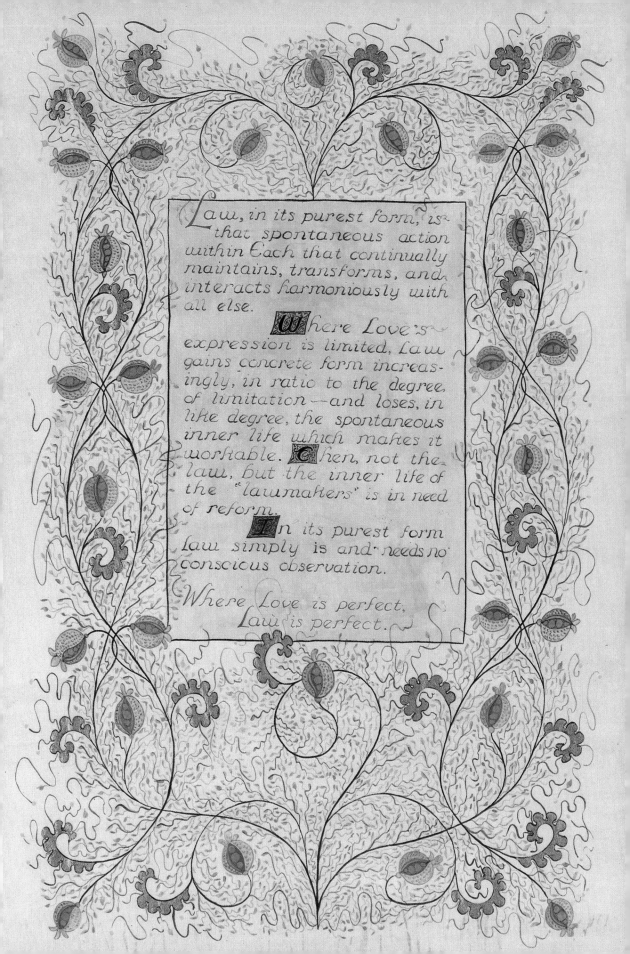

Law, in its purest form, is that spontaneous action within Each that continually maintains, transforms, and interacts harmoniously with all else.

Where Love's expression is limited, Law gains concrete form increasingly, in ratio to the degree of limitation — and loses, in like degree, the spontaneous inner life which makes it workable. Then, not the law, but the inner life of the "lawmakers" is in need of reform.

In its purest form law simply is and needs no conscious observation.

Where Love is perfect, Law is perfect.

M is for MOMENTS

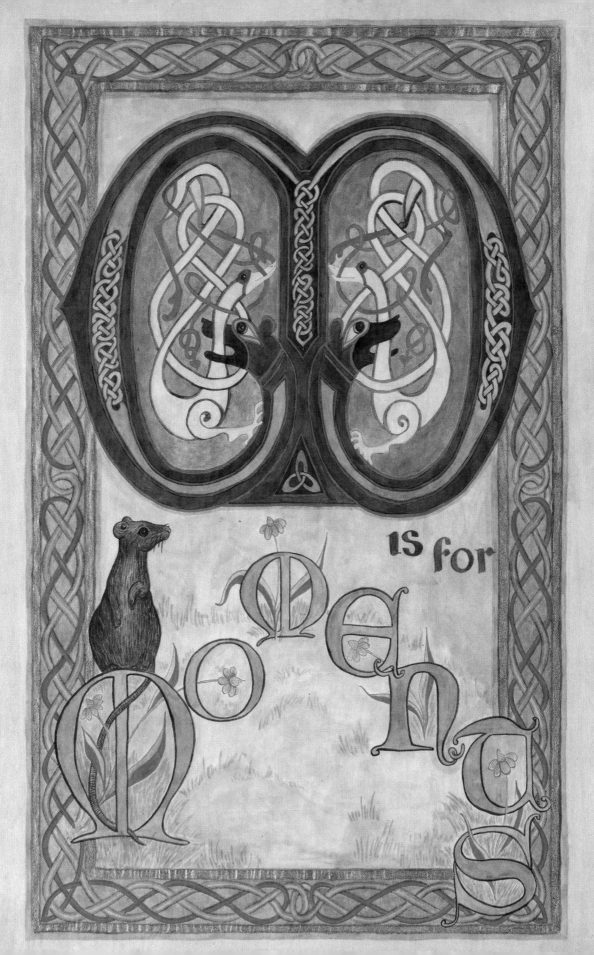

IS for

MONDAYS

Take good care of your MOMENTS and your milleniums will take care of themselves.

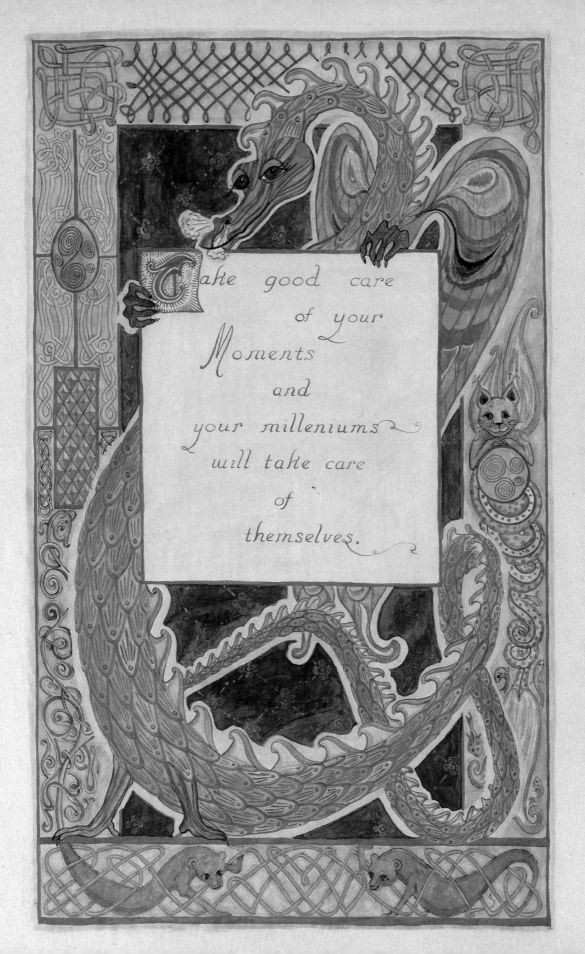

Take good care
of your
Moments
and
your milleniums
will take care
of
themselves.

N is for NOBILITY

NOBILITY depends, not on parentage or place of birth, but on breadth of compassion and depth of lovingkindness. If we would be noble, let us be great-hearted. The way is a hard journey, but the end is a wingèd crown.

Nobility depends, not on parentage or place of birth, but on breadth of compassion and depth of lovingkindness. If we would be noble, let us be great-hearted. The way is a hard journey, but the end is a wingèd crown.

O is for ORDER

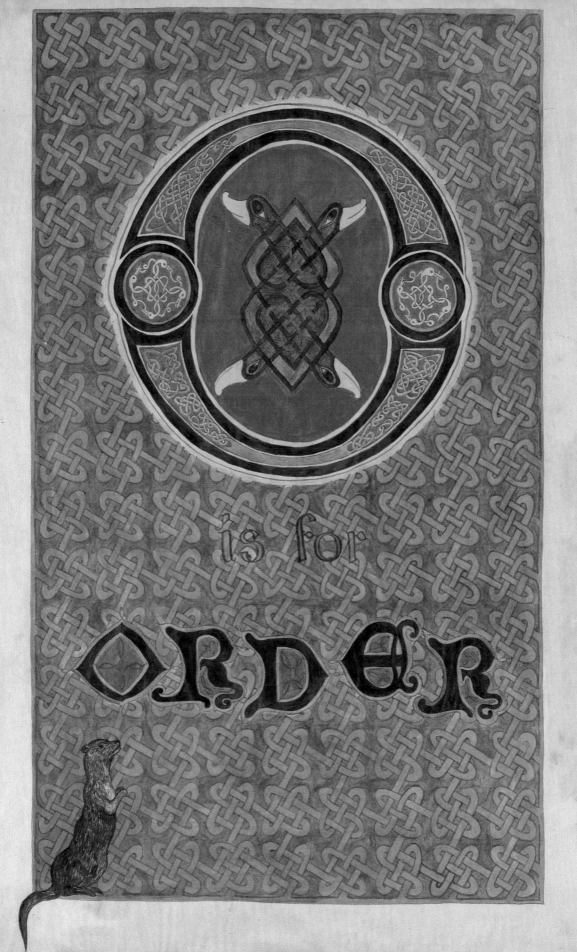

is for

ORDER

ORDER is a prime factor in the organization of Being. It is Being's means of freedom. Order is the framework which makes function possible; it is the seed of creativity.

God cannot cast the smallest spray of stardrops into night but they maintain His orderliness within, and move without in sweetest order with all else that is.

It is by means of order that we know the sweetness of life.

Order is a prime factor
in the organization of
Being. It is Being's
means of freedom. Order
is the framework which
makes function possible;
it is the seed of creativity.

God can-
not cast the smallest
spray of stardrops into
night but they maintain
His orderliness within,
and move without in
sweetest order with all
else that is.

It is by
means of order that we
know the sweetness of
life.

P is for PEARLS

is for

PEARLS

PEARLS are sea-gifts.

Many-layered, they glow with a lustre from within. The spiritual life is an Ocean of Many Treasures; its pearls are both plenteous and rare.

Those who dive deeply discover the Ocean's secrets; those who persevere find the rarest of them.

The Seekers of Divine Pearls shall not be disappointed.

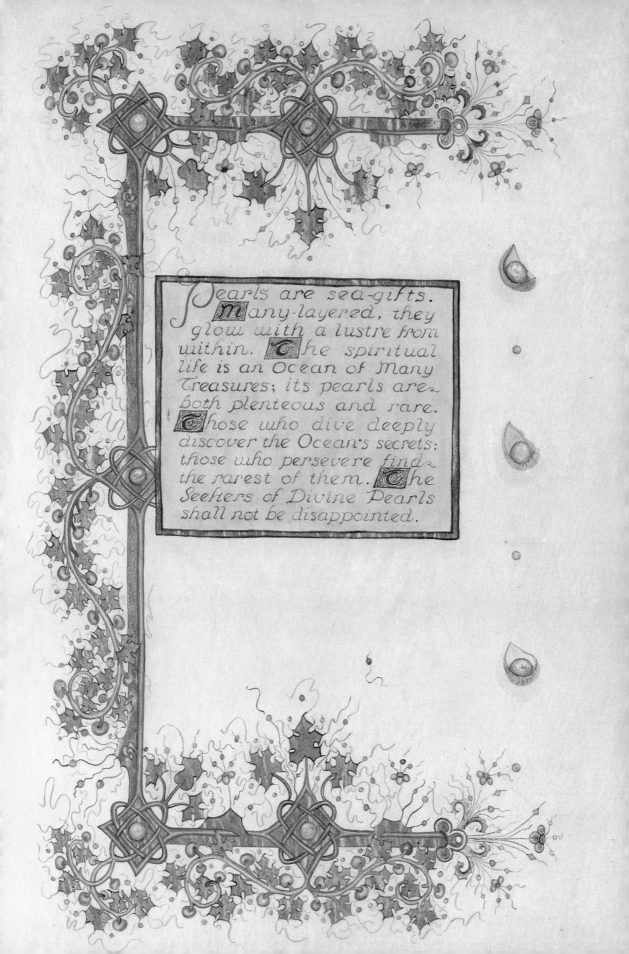

Pearls are sea-gifts. Many-layered, they glow with a lustre from within. The spiritual life is an Ocean of Many Treasures; its pearls are both plenteous and rare. Those who dive deeply discover the Ocean's secrets; those who persevere find the rarest of them. The Seekers of Divine Pearls shall not be disappointed.

Q is for QUEST

QUEST is the Way of the Spirit. It is the path upon which humankind is born. Even those blind to this truth pursue the path, unknowing. Even those who see and turn away can find no flight that bears not upon their quest.

We cannot be, except we seek our souls' fulfillment. We cannot seek but we shall find.

Quest is the Way of the Spirit. It is the path upon which humankind is born. Even those blind to this truth pursue the path, unknowing. Even those who see and turn away can find no flight that bears not upon their quest. We cannot be, except we seek our souls' fulfillment. We cannot seek but we shall find.

R is for RO-MLEN

R

is for

Ro-Mlen

RO-MLEN is not exactly a "name"; your closest word is "truth." But Ro-Mlen is neither noun nor verb. We do ro-mlen. . . . we are Ro-Mlen . . . we have nothing to offer except ro-mlen. Ro-Mlen is as a condition, and it is as the action that takes place within that condition, and it is as the fruit of that action. . .

Though not All-Truth, it is all-truthful, and it is great truth. It is as our particular shape-of-truth, given us by the Divine, a living child of The-One-Who-Is. It is a honey of heavenly sweetness—it is the one-and-many—it is the changing-and-remaining—

Ro-Mlen is as a poem spoken one day when God was in love. . . .

Ro-Mlen is not exactly a "name"; your closest word is "truth". But Ro-Mlen is neither noun nor verb. We do ro-mlen.... we are Ro-Mlen.... we have nothing to offer except ro-mlen. Ro-Mlen is as a condition, and it is as the action that takes place within that condition, and it is as the fruit of that action... Though not All-Truth, it is all-truthful, and it is great truth. It is as our particular shape-of-truth, given us by the Divine, a living child of The-One-Who-Is. It is a honey of heavenly sweetness — it is the one-and-many — it is the changing-and-remaining —

Ro-Mlen is as a poem spoken one day when God was in love....

S is for SILENCE

SILENCE is a gift of hidden wonders. By its power we hear the Song of Songs; at its core we find God.

Silence is not less than sound, but more. Silence is the sound of All-in-Unity.

In the shallows, on the sandbars, the Ocean is noisy. But those who seek the treasures of the deeps go in silence there.

God is found in the waiting silence of the seeking heart.

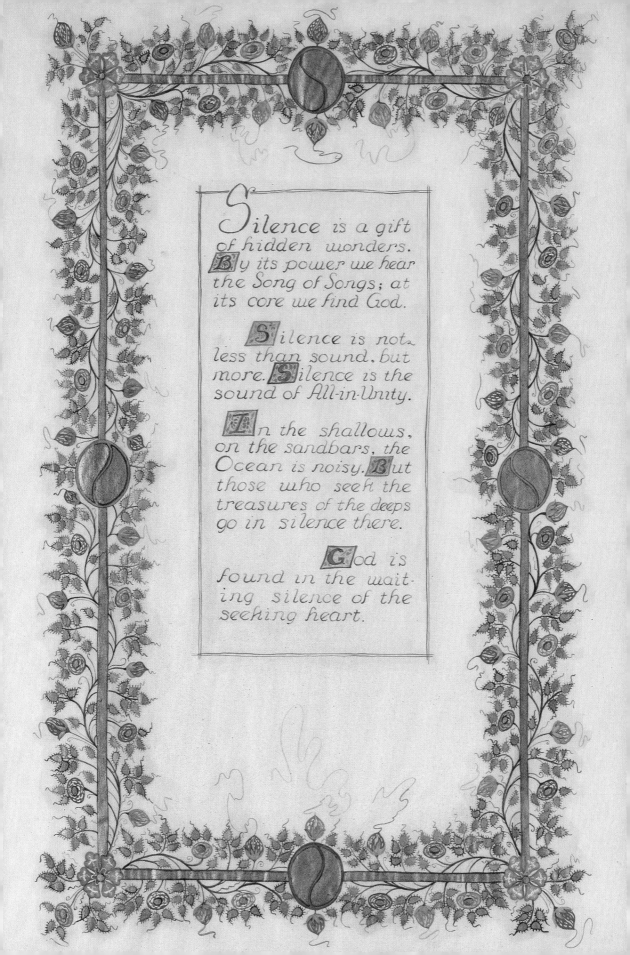

Silence is a gift
of hidden wonders.
By its power we hear
the Song of Songs; at
its core we find God.

Silence is not
less than sound, but
more. Silence is the
sound of All-in-Unity.

In the shallows,
on the sandbars, the
Ocean is noisy. But
those who seek the
treasures of the deeps
go in silence there.

God is
found in the wait-
ing silence of the
seeking heart.

T is for TIME

is for TIME

TIME, of itself, is neither long nor short, great nor small. It is only used or unused and cannot be anything else. Time's attributes are determined by usage, its nature is paradox. A thousand years are as a twinkling in the sight of God, yet in the space of a second man can experience the Divine.

Time is the timeless chalice into which the Divine has poured the wine of life. One may drink deep or shallow, as one will, but the cup changes not.

Those who seek the timeless shall have time for all that is necessary.

Time, of itself, is neither long nor short, great nor small. It is only used or unused and cannot be anything else. Time's attributes are determined by usage, its nature is paradox. A thousand years are as a twinkling in the sight of God, yet in the space of a second man can experience the Divine.

Time is the timeless chalice into which the Divine has poured the wine of life. One may drink deep or shallow, as one will, but the cup changes not.

Those who seek the timeless shall have time for all that is necessary.

U is for UNITY

is for

UNITY

UNITY is the beginning of all and the end of all; the Line-of-Diverse-Experiences curves to enclose the Circle-of-Unity.*

Before there was Each, All-That-Is was in unity; then came Each and Unity changed form to include diversity in its parts. Thus with the coming of creation the Unity-that-was not only ceased but increased, for the Divine All is such that It cannot give away but It have more in return—and It cannot grow less but it grow greater—and It cannot lose in unity but It gain in Unity.

Unity flowers for those who would love God, therefore seek ye through the veils for the Hidden-Heart-Within.

*sphere-of-unity

Unity is the beginning of all and the end of all; the Line-of-Diverse-Experiences curves to enclose the Circle-of-Unity.*

Before there was Each, All-That-Is was in unity; then came Each and Unity changed form to include diversity in its parts. Thus with the coming of creation the Unity-that-was not only ceased but increased, for the Divine All is such that It cannot give away but It have more in return — and It cannot grow less but it grow greater — and It cannot lose in unity but It gain in unity.

Unity flowers for those who would love God. Wherefore seek ye through the veils for the Hidden-Heart-Within.

*sphere-of-unity

V is for VERITIES

V is for VIRTUES

VERITIES come, from saint and prophet, like wingèd guides. Much can be learned from observation of their flight. But there are those who would capture and cage them, and these learn nothing from their observation except restriction and limitation.

There is no wisest saying that cannot be misapplied, for the truth of verities cannot be found in their letter but only in their spirit, and that spirit is not known outside of the soul's knowledge of self, of others, of All-That-Is.

All verity is paradox. One who would apply a verity before grasping its paradox is as one who would run up a flight of stairs using only the left foot and leaving the right foot behind.

Do not use verities to hone your mind but rather to purify your heart—for where the heart is pure the Divine Itself will enter with enlightenment.

Verities come, from saint and prophet, like wingèd guides. Much can be learned from observation of their flight. But there are those who would capture and cage them, and these learn nothing from their observation except restriction and limitation.

There is no wisest saying that cannot be misapplied, for the truth of verities cannot be found in their letter but only in their spirit, and that spirit is not known outside of the soul's knowledge of self, of others, of All-That-Is.

All verity is paradox. One who would apply a verity before grasping its paradox is as one who would run up a flight of stairs using only the left foot and leaving the right foot behind.

Do not use verities to hone your mind but rather to purify your heart—for where the heart is pure the Divine Itself will enter with enlightenment.

W is for WONDER

W is for
WONDER

WONDER is a dear daughter of All-That-Is. She stands before Creation in amazed delight, and Creation responds in kind. Wonder wastes no time on self-important calculation; the trials of her littleness do not offend her. Laughing, she runs to the arms of All-That-Is and does not fear rejection.

Wonder neither plots nor worries, she puts on no sophistications. Wisdom flowers in her attitudes and humility springs from her practices.

Those who look with wonder on all that is shall find the love of All-That-Is looking back on them with welcome.

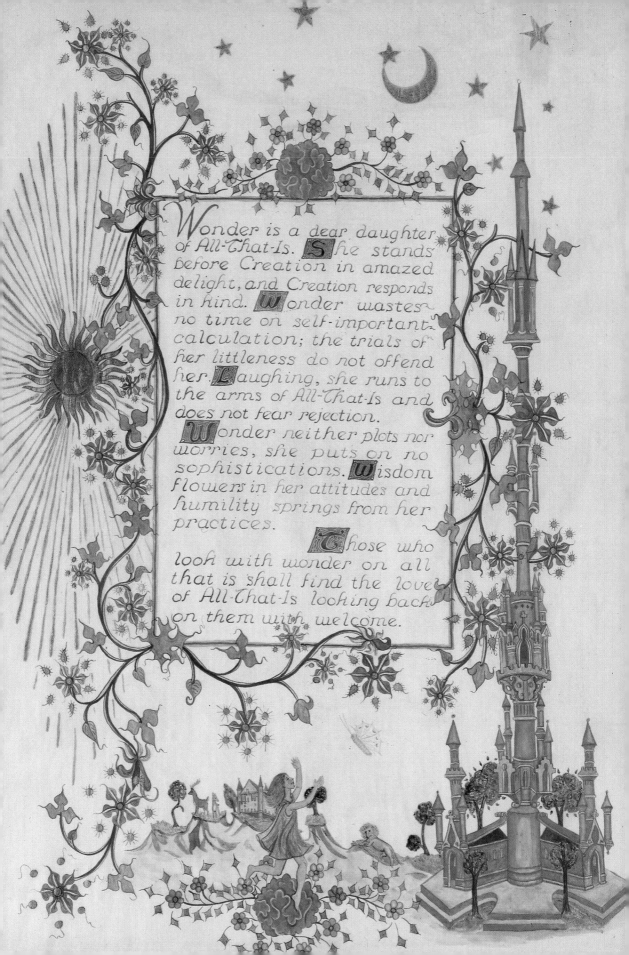

Wonder is a dear daughter of All-That-Is. She stands before Creation in amazed delight, and Creation responds in kind. Wonder wastes no time on self-important calculation; the trials of her littleness do not offend her. Laughing, she runs to the arms of All-That-Is and does not fear rejection. Wonder neither plots nor worries, she puts on no sophistications. Wisdom flowers in her attitudes and humility springs from her practices.

Those who look with wonder on all that is shall find the love of All-That-Is looking back on them with welcome.

℘ is for PARADOX

XODARAP-PARADOX is the stairway that comprehension climbs until once again Each understands All-That-Is. In any given spot we strive with conflicts but when we have embraced the differences we find ourselves on a higher step and, looking down, our souls understand the unity of all below that vantage point.

Contradiction and Paradox both contain "opposites," but contradiction is the point at which they are seen as being separated, and Paradox is the point of source, at which they are seen reconciled.

A Gift of Paradox is a Gift of Truth. If you seek to understand paradox you will come to understand the essence and nature of truth.

Robbing-paradox is the stairway that comprehension climbs until once again Each understands All-That-Is. In any given spot we strive with conflicts but when we have embraced the differences we find ourselves on a higher step and, looking down, our souls understand the unity of all below that vantage point.

Contradiction and Paradox both contain "opposites", but contradiction is the point at which they are seen as being separated, and Paradox is the point of source, at which they are seen reconciled.

A Gift of Paradox is a Gift of Truth. If you seek to understand paradox you will come to understand the essence and nature of truth.

Y is for YIELD

Y is for
YIELO

YIELD is the companion of strive. No striving bears good fruit unless accompanied by the right yielding that should go with it.

Many "failures" come from striving without also yielding—for there is more gain in giving than in grasping; and though the Cosmos *may* be caught by one who can run fast enough—for one who can stay still it is already at hand.

The Divine yielded to All-That-Is and creation was born. In the return of that act of yielding, that divine "yes" to life, Each knows again fulfillment.

You *are*, and you are *you*, because All-That-Is said, "Yes." Your "yes" to all that is shall yield your soul's fulfillment.

Yield is the companion of strive. No striving bears good fruit unless accompanied by the right yielding that should go with it.

Many "failures" come from striving without also yielding —for there is more gain in giving than in grasping; and though the Cosmos may be caught by one who can run fast enough —for one who can stay still it is already at hand.

The Divine yielded to All-That-Is and creation was born. In the return of that act of yielding, that divine "yes" to life, Each knows again fulfillment.

You are, and you are you, because All-That-Is said, "Yes." Your "yes" to all that is shall yield your soul's fulfillment.

Z is for ZENITH

is for

Zenith

The mountaintop,
the tallest tower,
the wave at crest,
the bud a'flower,
a silver realm,
a crystal door,
a'sharing bread
among the poor. . . .
ZENITH is
not end nor
beginning
but the sum of both
. . . and more . . .

Zenith is an idea. Never fear what ye shall find there, though the way seems sometimes fearful . . .

Where all the threads draw together and the tapestry stands whole—

What was stumbling block now cornerstone—

The barren tree abloom with its secret, wondrous fruit—

At the core of heart's desire, a reality.

And so it shall be, for All is Well and all is well, and thou shalt see it, that all is well.

The mountain top,
the tallest tower,
the wave at crest,
the bud a'flower,
a silver realm,
a crystal door,
a'sharing bread
among the poor.

...zenith is
not end nor
beginning
but the sum of both
...and more...

Zenith is an idea.
[N]ever fear what ye shall
find there, though the way
seems sometimes fearful...

Where all the threads draw together and
the tapestry stands whole —
What was stumbling block now cornerstone —
The barren tree abloom with its
secret, wondrous fruit —
At the core of heart's desire, a reality.

And so it shall be, for

All is Well and all is well,
and thou shalt see it,
that all is well.